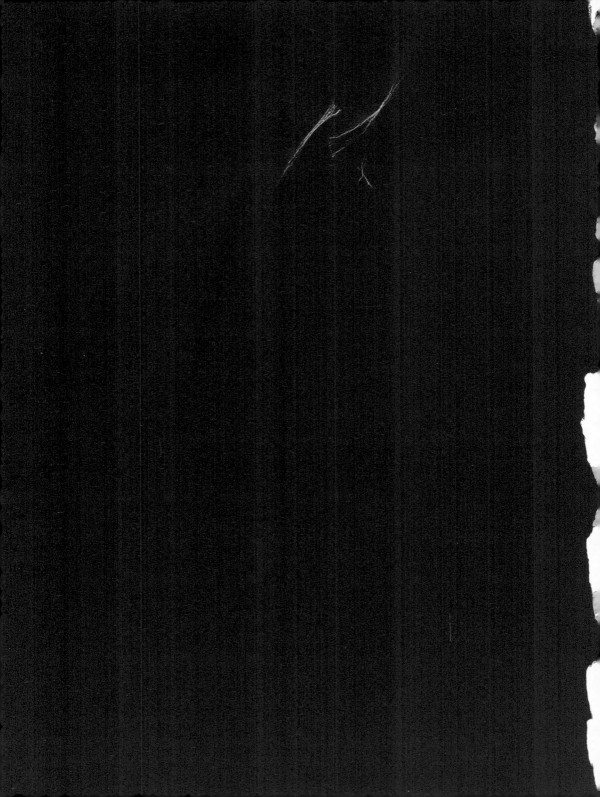

101

FASCINATING FACTS TO KNOW ABOUT

DINOSAURS

Editorial Director: Maria Jesús Díaz
Designer: Estelle Talavera
Author: Niko Dominguez
Editor: Susaeta
Illustrator: F. Valiente / Susaeta
Translated and edited by Lisa Regan

© SUSAETA EDICIONES, S.A. - Obra colectiva
C/ Campezo, 13 - 28022 Madrid
Tel.: 91 3009100 - 91 3009118
www.susaeta.com

English edition first published 2015 by Brown Watson
The Old Mill, 76 Fleckney Road
Kibworth Beauchamp
Leicestershire LE8 0HG

ISBN: 978-0-7097-2233-5

© 2015 Brown Watson, England

Printed in Malaysia

101

FASCINATING FACTS TO KNOW ABOUT

DINOSAURS

Brown Watson

ENGLAND

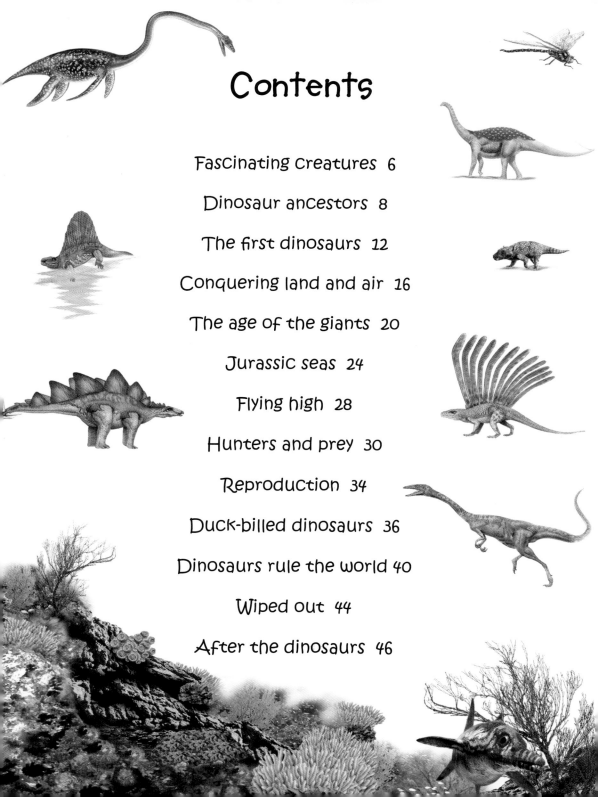

Contents

Fascinating creatures

1 Do you know how long dinosaurs existed on our planet? They were around for an amazing 165 million years!

During this time, dinosaurs evolved to have a variety of forms, with huge differences in size, appearance and habits. Some were as big as a building, while others were as small as a rabbit. Some ran on their two back legs and others walked on all fours. There were meat-eaters, plant-eaters, dinosaurs with feathers, scales, horns, a beak, claws and spikes. True dinosaurs had certain things in common: they were land-dwelling creatures that laid eggs; most of them had three toes; and almost all of them had tough, scaly skin.

2 We can't be sure how many dinosaur species existed.

Over 500 types have been found and named, but not all of these are based on complete skeletons. They are divided into two main types, depending on their hip joints: saurischians (lizard hipped) and ornithischians (bird hipped).

Dinosaur ancestors

3 During the Permian Period, about 300 million years ago, the seas receded and the shallower lakes disappeared.

With more land and less water, the planet became a place of forests and deserts. Some animals, especially reptiles, adapted to live on the land, and new types of plants appeared.

MILLERETA was a reptile that looked like a large lizard. It measured around 60 cm and probably ate insects.

4 Mammal—like reptiles extended far and wide, and at the end of the Permian Period they dominated the planet.

These creatures were pelycosaurs, part of the synapsid group with a characteristic hole in their skull, like Dimetrodon. This giant predator had a narrow body and long tail, with a large sail on its back. It may have used this to regulate its body temperature.

DIMETRODON lived at least 40 million years before the dinosaurs. It was one of the first reptiles to have a sail on its back.

5 Archosaurs spread around the whole planet.

These reptiles were the direct ancestors of dinosaurs and pterosaurs, but also of creatures that are still alive today, such as birds and crocodiles.

6 The Permian was the last period in the Paleozoic Era.

The Paleozoic began 542 million years ago and lasted until 251 million years ago. At the start, all living things were in the water. By the end of the era, reptiles dominated the planet and the first modern plants had appeared.

7 Proterosuchus looked very similar to modern-day crocodiles.

It is thought that it would lie in wait under the water, and leap out to grab creatures at the water's edge as they drank.

PROTEROSUCHUS had strong, powerful jaws for attacking large creatures.

8 Gorgonopsians were the main meat-eaters of the late Permian Period.

They had long, leaf-shaped canine teeth and tremendously strong incisors for biting. Some of these creatures grew to the size of a small rhinoceros.

DID YOU KNOW...?

Scientists have discovered that birds, rather than reptiles, are the closest descendants of dinosaurs.

9 Pareiasaurus had strong legs like an elephant's.

Pareiasaurus was a plant-eater that lived amongst low-lying plants. It had powerful legs that stuck out at the sides, like those of a reptile. Its teeth were jagged for chewing tough vegetation. It even had teeth on the roof of its mouth!

10 The Permian Period is named after an area in Russia called Perm Krai.

The region is near the Ural Mountains, and many discoveries relating to the period have been found here.

PAREIASAURUS, despite its large size, was a peaceful plant-eating reptile.

Its back was protected by lots of bony plates on its skin.

11 In this period, some amphibians evolved into reptiles.

Their eggs changed and they were able to breed out of the water, with no need for the tadpole stage that amphibians still have today.

12 The Permian Period ended with a mass extinction that wiped out many species.

Scientists are not exactly sure what caused it, but around 90% of marine species and 70% of land animals were lost.

DIICTODON had a beak, with two large curved tusks at the sides.

13 Diictodon was a tiny, plant—eating creature.

It lived in the desert and semi-desert, and built tunnels to protect itself from predators and from the extreme heat.

11

The first dinosaurs

14 At the start of the Mesozoic Era, during the Triassic Period, the land was joined in one giant continent, surrounded by sea. This supercontinent was called Pangaea.

The climate was hot and dry, and animals could roam wherever they wanted. This is when the first dinosaurs, such as Eoraptor and Coelophysis, appeared.

15 Fast hunter

The teeth of Coelophysis were sharp and jagged so that it could eat small lizards.

CYNOGNATHUS

16 Cynognathus: a prehistoric dog!

It had two sharp fangs for attacking its prey, and cheek teeth to help it chew. It was not a dinosaur but a cynodont (mammal–like reptile).

17 Postosuchus was a deadly predator.

It had a body like a crocodile and legs that were typical of a dinosaur. It hunted its prey in the vast Triassic semi-deserts, ambushing them and taking them by surprise.

18 Not as fast as later dinosaurs...

Early dinosaurs had legs that stuck out at the sides, like those of a lizard, which made them much slower than the dinosaurs that followed in the Jurassic and Cretaceous Periods.

POSTOSUCHUS

19 The oldest known dinosaur is Eoraptor, or the 'dawn thief'.

It gets its name because it marks the dawning of the dinosaur age. Eoraptor was as small as some dogs, but was a fearsome predator, fast and clever.

EORAPTOR ran with its tail held out stiffly to give it extra balance.

DRAGONFLIES have been around since prehistoric times, and lived alongside the dinosaurs!

20 Lystrosaurus survived the massive extinction that happened at the end of the Permian age.

It measured around a metre and weighed 100 kg. This herbivore had sturdy legs, and was about the size of a pig. It made underground burrows and was by far the most common land vertebrate of the early Triassic.

LYSTROSAURUS means 'shovel lizard'.

COELOPHYSIS was a fast-moving predator which probably lived in herds.

21 The speedy, agile Coelophysis ('hollow form') had dozens of saw-like teeth.

Its bones were hollo making it lighter so it could run fast to catch its prey.

22 Theropods were the dominant hunters on land until they went extinct.

They made up a large and diverse group, but were all carnivorous and walked on two legs.

DID YOU KNOW...?

Paleontologists are scientists who investigate early life on Earth by studying fossil remains.

23 Staurikosaurus ('Southern Cross lizard') was one of the first dinosaurs found in the southern hemisphere.

Measuring around two metres, it chased small reptiles with its five-fingered 'hands'.

Conquering land and air

24
During the Triassic period, most creatures lived near the sea.

The middle of the continent was made up of huge deserts and dry areas where only certain specialised animals could survive.

25
In the past, in places like China and Scotland, dinosaur fossils were sometimes thought to be the remains of dragons.

The word dinosaur comes from the Greek *deinos*, which means 'terrible', and *sauros*, which means 'lizard'.

EDAPHOSAURUS means 'pavement lizard'.

PLATEOSAURUS

26 Plateosaurus was the first of the large plant–eaters.

It was much bigger than a bus and so was able to reach leaves high up in the trees, without competition from other plant–eaters. For this reason, it survived for many years.

27 Throughout the Triassic period, most of the Himalayas were under the sea.

The skeleton of an enormous sea-going ichthyosaur was found in Tibet, now 4,800 metres above sea level!

28 In the Triassic period, the vegetation was lush, leafy plants with no flowers.

Mosses and liverworts (with no stems or roots) were the main plants in wet areas. Tall plants and giant ferns grew to be as much as 30 metres high. Early dinosaurs would have fed on this soft foliage.

29 Pterosaurs were the earliest vertebrates to develop powered flight.

They existed for a long span of time, from 228 to 66 million years ago. Pterosaurs ranged in size, from ones as small as a sparrow to some as large as planes.

PTEROSAUR
or 'winged lizard'.

30 A pterosaur's wings didn't have any feathers.

They were thin and made of skin, stretched out by an extremely long fourth finger.

31 Eudimorphodon is the earliest known pterosaur.

It lived by the coast and flew low over the water to catch fish. At the end of its long tail was a diamond-shaped flap which acted like a rudder, helping it to steer and manoeuvre in the air.

The wings of EUDIMORPHODON could be a metre across.

32 Longisquama was an extraordinary looking reptile.

Not many remains have been found, but it appears to have had long, coloured scales sticking up from its back.

33 Dilophosaurus had a very unusual feature.

It had two bony crests on its skull, that looked like plates standing to drain in a rack! It lived in the early Jurassic Period, and was one of the bigger meat-eaters of this time, reaching around 6 metres long.

34 Don't believe everything you see!

The Dilophosaurus characters on screen, in movies such as *Jurassic Park*, aren't based on real findings. It probably didn't have a neck frill, and almost certainly didn't spit poison!

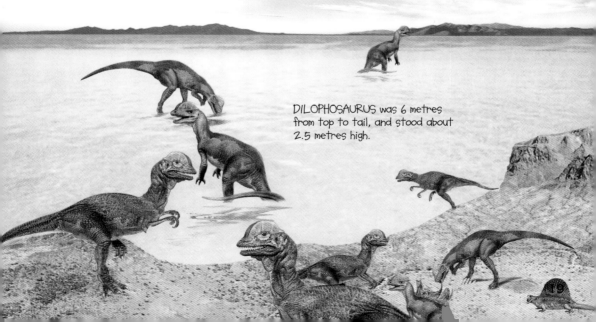

DILOPHOSAURUS was 6 metres from top to tail, and stood about 2.5 metres high.

The age of the giants

35 During the Jurassic Period, the woods were filled with plant-eating dinosaurs of all sizes.

The world changed yet again, and an increase in rainfall led to a much greener planet. The continents began to form and the climate in general was hot and humid, allowing lush forests and jungles to appear. Ferns and conifers were in abundance.

SALTASAURUS means 'lizard from Salta'. It had bony plates in the skin on its back.

BRACHIOSAURUS had front legs longer than its back legs, making it resemble the modern giraffe. It was much bigger though!

36 Competition for plants to eat was fierce, so the plant-eaters grew bigger.

Brachiosaurus was enormous. By stretching its long neck it could reach leaves up to 9 metres off the ground. That's three storeys high!

37 As plant-eaters grew larger, so did their predators.

The most impressive of the meat-eaters was Allosaurus, which was 12 metres long and weighed 2 tonnes. It walked on two legs, and its claws and teeth were ferocious.

ALLOSAURUS, 'different lizard', preyed on other large dinosaurs.

38 Not all dinosaurs were enormous at this time.

The giants get the most attention, but there were many smaller ones. Some dinosaurs of the Jurassic Period developed heavy armour as protection, like Dracopelta, which was 2 metres long, and Stegosaurus, which reached 9 metres.

39 The largest dinosaur footprint found is 1.5 metres across!

Imagine having a footprint the size of a car! Its owner is estimated to have weighed around 40 tonnes and been 25 metres long – the size of a tennis court!

40 Mamenchisaurus was a giant herbivore that reached 35 metres long.

Over half of that length was its extremely long neck!

ARCHAEOPTERYX, or 'ancient feather', is the oldest known bird.

SEISMOSAURUS

41 The biggest carnivores were fairly slow.

Instead of using speed, they were good at tracking. They followed their prey without being spotted, and then launched a surprise attack, before their prey could make their escape.

42 Some dinosaurs are discovered and then disappear again when more is known about them.

When it was first found, Seismosaurus was thought to have measured 40 metres long and weighed over 25 tonnes. Scientists examining the bones re-evaluated it and decided it was actually much smaller. These days, many think it was actually a sub-species of the well-known Diplodocus.

The gentle giant SALTASAURUS could eat from high branches.

43 Even giants have to defend themselves.

Growing huge allowed dinosaurs to reach the highest leaves, but was also a good way to deter predators. Some smaller plant-eaters had tough scales to help defend themselves.

DID YOU KNOW...?

Giant dinosaurs also laid giant eggs, which could be up to 30 cm long.

44 One of the best known giants is Diplodocus.

It needed large amounts of food so ate almost constantly, moving its head and long neck from side to side.

DIPLODOCUS used its long tail like a whip to keep predators at a safe distance.

Jurassic seas

45 Ichthyosaurs ruled the deepest parts of the oceans for most of the Triassic and Jurassic Periods.

These large marine reptiles looked similar to the dolphins of today. They could swim up to 40 km/h and they fed on fish, shellfish and other sea creatures, but although they were reptiles, they gave birth to live young like mammals do. They were the rulers of the seas until the plesiosaurs came along...

LIOPLEURODON
was a fierce predator.

46 Liopleurodon grew
between 5 and 7 metres long.

It was a powerful plesiosaur that could
swim fast in short bursts, accelerating
towards its prey and leaving its
victim no time to escape
its enormous jaws.

47 During the Jurassic Period, Pangaea broke into smaller sections.

As the dinosaurs dominated other species, Pangaea split into two continents: Laurasia and Gondwana. In between, great oceans teemed with life.

ELASMOSAURUS may have inspired the legend of the Loch Ness Monster.

The Jurassic Period gets its name from the Jura Mountains, on the border of France and Switzerland, which were formed at this time.

48 Longest neck

Elasmosaurus was a plesiosaur with an extremely long neck. It had over 70 neck bones, more than any other known creature.

49 Ichthyosaurs were carnivorous reptiles. They would come to the surface to fill their lungs with air and then dive into the depths.

They became extinct in the middle of the Cretaceous Period, when plesiosaurs replaced them as the top marine predators.

The first complete ICHTHYOSAUR skeletons were found in England in the early 1800s.

50 Plesiosaurs were divided into two groups.

Some, like Elasmosaurus, had a long neck and small head, and legs like oars. Pliosaurs like Liopleurodon had a short neck, large head and very strong jaws. They could crush shells and bones easily.

CRYPTOCLIDUS was a plesiosaur that measured 3 to 8 metres and weighed about 8 tonnes.

51 Ammonites were the ancestors of octopus, squid and cuttlefish.

There were also jellyfish and nautilus in the oceans, like the ones alive today.

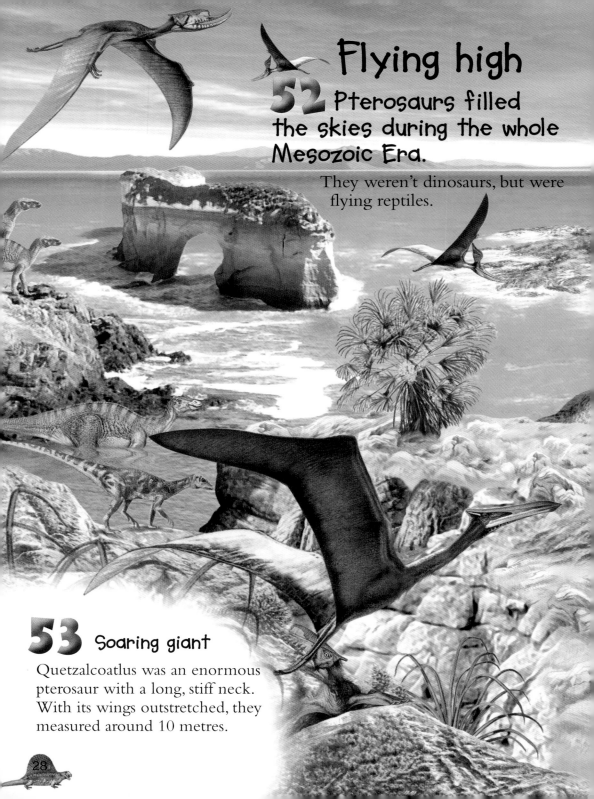

Flying high

52 Pterosaurs filled the skies during the whole Mesozoic Era.

They weren't dinosaurs, but were flying reptiles.

53 Soaring giant

Quetzalcoatlus was an enormous pterosaur with a long, stiff neck. With its wings outstretched, they measured around 10 metres.

DSUNGARIPTERUS

54 Pterosaurs looked a lot like birds.

They flapped their wings to fly, laid eggs, and had good eyesight, just like modern birds. But they were reptiles, with teeth, large brains, and probably did not have feathers.

55 Dsungaripterus had a pointed beak that curved upwards.

It poked around in the sand and mud to find worms and molluscs. It also had a peculiar head crest.

56 Tropeognathus or 'keel-snout'.

Its peculiar snout was tipped with a keel like the bottom of a boat.

TROPEOGNATHUS

Hunters and prey

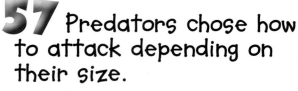

PISANOSAURUS grew to around 1 metre long.

57 Predators chose how to attack depending on their size.

The smaller ones were fast with sharp teeth; bigger ones could rely on their brute strength and sharp claws.

58 Small dinosaurs lived alongside the large ones, but survived on a different diet.

Some dinosaurs have been discovered that were as small as a chicken or a cat. They were speedy hunters that gobbled up insects and worms. They ran around on two legs, probably keeping out of the way of the bigger dinosaurs.

59 Pelecanimimus looked a little like a modern pelican.

It had a throat pouch which it may have used to store fish. It had a huge number of teeth; scientists think 220 in total!

PELECANIMIMUS was small – around 2 metres long.

60 The smallest dinosaurs had only one defence: speed.

One example is Hypsilophodon: it lived in small herds, roamed the forests and used its stiff tail for balance when it ran at top speed to escape from a predator.

HYPSILOPHODON had a horny beak for eating plants.

61 Ornitholestes was a small dinosaur that ate many different creatures.

It would have preyed upon newborn dinosaur babies, as well as lizards, frogs, and early mammals that were around at this time. It probably had a covering of fur-like feathers on its body.

COMPSOGNATHUS was the size of a hen. We know it ate lizards because its stomach contents were preserved in fossils.

CARNOTAURUS ate other smaller dinosaurs.

62 Carnotaurus, one of the biggest predatory dinosaurs, had two small horns over its eyes.

They could have been used for fighting other members of its species. Its name is related to these horns and means 'meat-eating bull'.

63 Even the most fierce, mighty dinosaurs could become prey to other hunters.

Small dinosaurs may have hunted in packs, ganging up on large dinosaurs. Their combined efforts meant they could take down prey much larger than themselves.

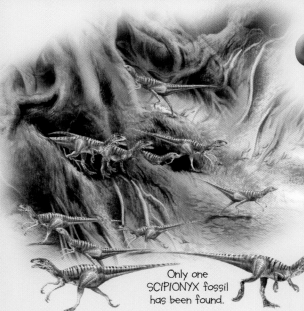

64 Hesperonychus was a small predator, probably with feathers on its body and its long tail.

It was the smallest carnivore found in North America, and is thought to have lived in the treetops and been able to glide.

Only one SCIPIONYX fossil has been found.

65 Micropachycephalosaurus holds two records in the world of the dinosaurs.

It was the smallest known dinosaur, but it also has the longest name! It weighed between 2 and 5 kg and was about the size of a small dog.

DID YOU KNOW…?

Large dinosaur eggs were rare. If they were too big, the shell would have to be so thick that the newborn would struggle to break out of it.

66 Heterodontosaurus had three different types of teeth.

Most dinosaurs had just one kind of tooth, but Heterodontosaurus had teeth for biting and different teeth for chewing. It also had a large pair of tusks. It could eat soft leaves and harder plant foods like buds and stems.

Reproduction

67 Scientists think that dinosaurs had mating rituals.

The males probably used their crests for attracting females, and might have carried out courting dances or even fought each other. They would have also had mating calls, like many species do today.

68 Baby dinosaurs hatched in nests, and probably stayed there while they were very young.

Their parents brought them food, in the same way that birds do with their chicks.

Paleontologists have found fossilised nests belonging to dinosaurs such as MAIASAURA.

69 Maiasaura built their nests together.

They raised their young in nesting colonies, like modern seabirds. Together, they could guard against predators and thieves trying to steal the eggs. Its name means 'caring mother lizard'. The babies grew from around 40 to 140 cm in a year.

70 The largest dinosaur eggs found so far measure a maximum of 30 cm.

They are from the giant sauropods, and have been found in a line not a nest, suggesting they may have been laid while the dinosaur was walking.

Duck-billed dinosaurs

71 Hadrosaurs were plant-eaters and had an unusual flattened jaw like a beak.

Many of them also had a hollow crest on their head. They lived in herds so that they could care for their young and protect each other from predators.

72 These dinosaurs had teeth at the back of their mouth for grinding food.

Hadrosaurs fed on low-level plants, and were the most common dinosaurs at the end of the Cretaceous Period.

HYPSILOPHODON was small and agile. It had a sharp beak and a pointed head.

73 'Thick-headed lizard'

Pachycephalosaurus was a herbivore that lived in herds. The top of its skull could be 23 cm thick, but it was probably not used for headbutting as was once thought.

PACHYCEPHALOSAURUS

Bulky body

The name hadrosaur means 'bulky body' and they did indeed have a
thick, chunky middle section and a massive stiff tail.

75 Parasaurolophus had an enormous hollow crest on its head.

The crest contained tubes that were linked to its nostrils. It could have used it to make sounds, for communication, or to help it identify other members of its species. It may also have helped it to control its body temperature.

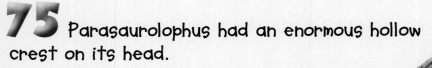

PARASAUROLOPHUS had a narrower beak than some other duck-billed dinosaurs.

EDMONTOSAURUS lived at the same time as Tyrannosaurus rex.

76 Browsing or grazing?

Large herds of hadrosaurs would roam the lands, in much the same way as herds of cattle, sheep or deer do now. They may have constantly grazed at ground level, or browsed, nibbling at shoots and leaves.

77 A hatchet-shaped crest

Lambeosaurus had an unusually shaped crest that sat at the front of its head. It was still thought to be used for making sounds and recognition. This dinosaur had over 100 teeth but only some of them were used at one time, with the others there to replace them as they fell out.

78 Edmontosaurus left useful fossils for paleontologists.

Most fossils are of hard substances like bones, but some Edmontosaurus fossils had skin impressions allowing us to learn more about their leathery exterior.

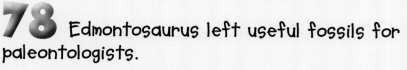

79 Hands and hooves

Hadrosaurs generally had mitten-like hands. Their feet had hard pads on the underside, a bit like a modern-day camel's, with hard hoof-like nails on them.

80 Safe and sound

Corythosaurus could make a loud, low noise with its head crest, probably similar to the sound of a trombone. It had a better sense of hearing than some dinosaurs, alerting it to the presence of danger, or to the calls of other members of its herd.

Dinosaurs rule the world

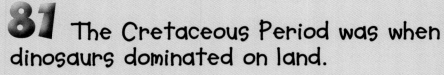

81 The Cretaceous Period was when dinosaurs dominated on land.

There was a wide variety of dinosaurs, which had evolved to adapt to the various environments they lived in. They were powerful and widespread, and were the top creatures on dry land.

82 Horns, armour and impressive claws: plant–eaters knew how to defend themselves.

Euoplocephalus was armoured all over its chunky body, and had a mace-shaped club at the end of its tail. It could even defend itself against a Tyrannosaurus rex. Triceratops, on the other hand, had a spikier attack: three giant horns on its head. Something for its enemies to think about!

83 The speedy Oviraptor or 'egg thief'

Its fossil was discovered on a nest of eggs, leading to the belief that it stole and ate eggs. It is more likely that the nest was its own and it was brooding the eggs.

84 Iguanodon lived in the early Cretaceous Period.

When first discovered, it caused some problems for paleontologists. They found a conical spiked fossil and thought it was a nose horn. It was later moved on skeleton models when they realised it was actually a spiked thumb!

DID YOU KNOW...?

Dinosaurs became extinct at the end of the Cretaceous Period, when they were at their most dominant.

85 Triceratops was a mighty beast, built like a tank, with added spikes!

It had a bony neck frill and three large horns; two on its forehead measuring up to a metre, and a smaller one on its snout. Despite its appearance, it was a gentle plant-eater and only used its weapons to defend itself from predators. It lived in herds.

86 Tyrannosaurus was the king of the dinosaurs, with large teeth and powerful jaws.

It was huge and fierce. It preyed on plant-eating dinosaurs but also on smaller carnivores. It stood 6 metres tall and was 12 metres from head to tail, with sharp claws and a gigantic mouth full of sharp teeth that could be up to 30 cm long.

87 Scavenger or fearsome hunter?

Tyrannosaurus rex probably fed in different ways, both attacking and killing its own prey, and scavenging food that other dinosaurs had already killed.

TYRANNOSAURUS REX means 'tyrant lizard king'.

88 Styracosaurus was, without doubt, one of the most striking in appearance.

It had a long, sharp horn on its snout, two small horns above its eyes, and an impressive frill behind its head that was edged with spikes of various sizes. This could have been for display to attract a mate and impress its rivals.

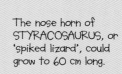

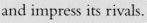

The nose horn of STYRACOSAURUS, or 'spiked lizard', could grow to 60 cm long.

90 Tough teeth

Many dinosaur teeth fossils have been found. They are even harder than bone, so fossilise well. Tyrannosaurus rex had different shaped teeth for tearing off lumps of flesh and for chewing and crushing bone and flesh.

89 Euoplocephalus was the most heavily armoured of the dinosaurs, with bony plates over its whole body.

It would have been hard to find any weak spot to attack, except maybe its underside, but it was low-slung and stood on four sturdy legs, so it wouldn't easily tip over! Even its eyelids were armoured!

The largest of the PTEROSAURS evolved in the Cretaceous Period.

Wiped out

91 Scientists cannot be certain what caused the extinction of dinosaurs and other species.

All they know for sure is that, 65 million years ago, over half of the world's plants and creatures were wiped out. Their main theories are that an asteroid or a series of volcanic eruptions changed the atmosphere and broke down the food chain.

92 Either of these events would have filled the skies with dust and blocked out light from the sun.

Layers of rock from 65 million years ago are rich in iridium, an element that is found in meteorites and also in magma from volcanic eruptions.

93 Creatures did not all die out at once, but gradually disappeared.

The lack of light would have killed many plants, so herbivores were left with nothing to eat. As they died out, the carnivores began to go hungry. But these are only theories: scientists constantly debate what happened.

HUNGAROSAURUS
had a row of spikes
along its back.

94 It wasn't just the dinosaurs that disappeared.

Other large creatures, like the pterosaurs and plesiosaurs, also fell victim to the mass extinction.

95 Dying plants

Whatever caused the extinction, it had a great effect on plants as well as animals. The dark skies prevented photosynthesis, which plants need to survive.

96 There have been some crazy theories about why the extinction happened.

It was suggested that dinosaurs were abducted by aliens, or that they just got bored and gave up trying to survive!

45

After the dinosaurs

97 Not everything died out in the extinction event 65 million years ago.

Representatives of many forms of life survived: insects, reptiles, birds, mammals, fish. They have made it possible for us to have the huge diversity of creatures we share our planet with today.

98 Mammals took over as king.

Many small creatures survived, possibly by burrowing underground to avoid the toxic, dust-filled atmosphere, and by eating insects which seemed unaffected by the events. Mammals gradually evolved and became larger.

99 Dinosaurs do still exist — in the form of birds.

Birds are the descendents of a certain type of dinosaur — the two-legged theropods such as Compsognathus. It is thought that they were small and resilient enough to survive and adapt to the new conditions on the planet, and over time have evolved into birds.

100 Fern frenzy

Many plants died but ferns thrived in the new environment, spreading rapidly. It took hundreds of thousands of years for forests to reappear.

101 Triceratops – the last of the dinosaurs?

The youngest fossils found, closest to the extinction date, are those of a Triceratops, uncovered in the USA.

Index